Festivals of the World

IRELAND

Gareth Stevens Publishing
MILWAUKEE

Written by
PATRICIA MCKAY

Edited by
SUSAN MCKAY

Designed by
HASNAH MOHD ESA

Picture research by
SUSAN JANE MANUEL

First published in North America in 1998 by
Gareth Stevens Publishing
1555 North River Center Drive, Suite 201
Milwaukee, Wisconsin 53212 USA

For a free color catalog describing Gareth
Stevens' list of high-quality books and multimedia
programs, call
1-800-542-2595 (USA)
or 1-800-461-9120 (Canada).
Gareth Stevens Publishing's Fax: (414) 225-0377.

© TIMES EDITIONS PTE. LTD. 1998
REPRINTED 2000
Originated and designed by
Times Books International
an imprint of Times Editions Pte. Ltd.
Times Centre, 1 New Industrial Road
Singapore 536196
E-mail: te@corp.tpl.com.sg
Printed in Malaysia

Library of Congress Cataloging-in-Publication Data:
McKay, Patricia.
Ireland / by Patricia McKay.
p. cm.—(Festivals of the world)
Includes bibliographical references and index.
Summary: Describes how the culture of Ireland is
reflected in its many festivals, including Saint
Brigid's Day, Puck's Fair, and Orange Day.
ISBN 0-8368-2004-5 (lib. bdg.)
1.Festivals—Ireland—Juvenile literature. 2
Ireland—Social life and customs—Juvenile
literature. [1. Festivals—Ireland. 2. Holidays—
Ireland. 3. Ireland—Social life and customs.] I.
Title. II. Series.
GT4847.5.A2M35 1998
394.269415—dc21   97-31588

2 3 4 5 6 7 8 9 04 03 02 01 00

CONTENTS

It's Festival Time . . .

Both pagan and Christian festivals are celebrated with much gaiety in Ireland. Irish festivals are famous for their music, storytelling, games, and dressing up. Come get dizzy dancing around a maypole, crown a goat at Puck's Fair, or kick up your heels at a gypsy campfire. It's festival time in Ireland . . .

WHERE'S IRELAND?

I reland is an island in Western Europe. The island is divided in two parts: Northern Ireland, which has ties with England, and the Republic of Ireland.

Rain from the Atlantic Ocean blows across the island, making it green both in summer and winter. For this reason, Ireland is often called the Emerald Isle. Along the western coast are mountains, which the Irish call reeks. There are also lots of lakes called loughs [lahks].

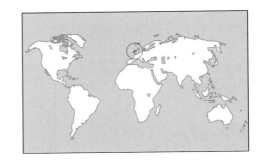

Who are the Irish?

In 450 B.C., **Celts** [kelts] from Middle Europe moved across the oceans to settle in Ireland. They believed in many gods. They also believed in little people, such as fairies, elves, and **leprechauns**.

After the birth of Christ, traders and soldiers arrived from Rome and introduced Christianity to the island.

In the last century, a disease attacked the potato crops and about one million people starved to death. More than one million Irish left the country to make their homes in England, Scotland, Canada, and the United States. They took their customs and beliefs with them. Do you have a friend or neighbor whose ancestors lived in Ireland?

A smiling Irish girl. Look at her lovely red hair!

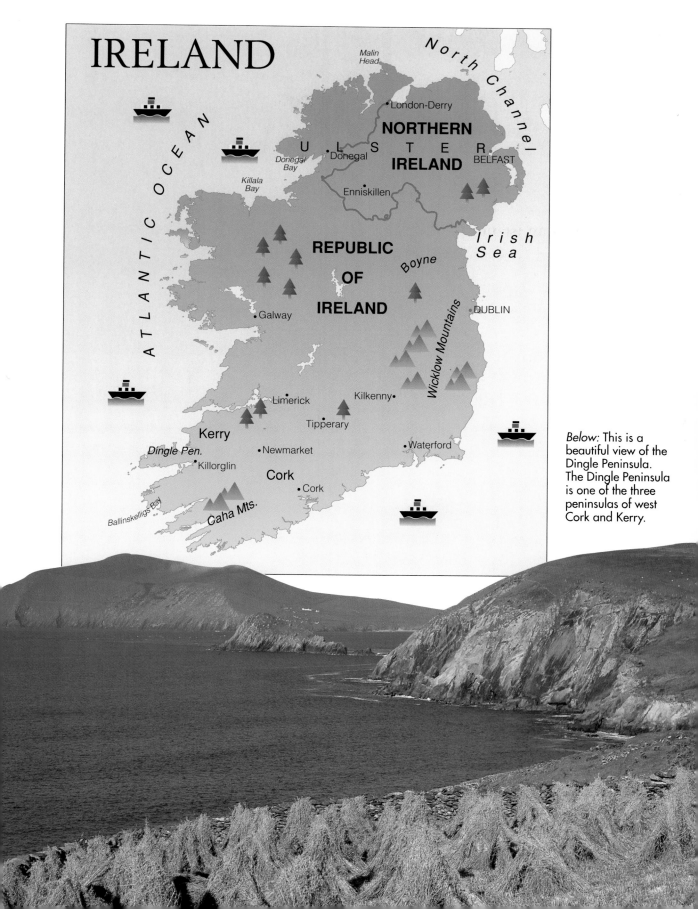

IRELAND

Malin Head

North Channel

• London-Derry

NORTHERN

U L S T E R

• Donegal

IRELAND

Donegal Bay

Killala Bay

• Enniskillen

BELFAST

REPUBLIC

Irish Sea

Boyne

OF

IRELAND

DUBLIN

Wicklow Mountains

• Galway

ATLANTIC OCEAN

Kilkenny •

Limerick

Kerry

Tipperary

Dingle Pen.

• Newmarket

• Waterford

• Killorglin

Cork

• Cork

Ballinskelligs Bay

Caha Mts.

Below: This is a beautiful view of the Dingle Peninsula. The Dingle Peninsula is one of the three peninsulas of west Cork and Kerry.

When's the Celebration?

SPRING

- **CHALK SUNDAY** (The first Sunday of Lent)—Unmarried people are marked with chalk as they enter the church. Traditionally, Catholics were not allowed to marry during Lent, so they had to wait until after Easter. Marking them with chalk is a way of teasing them for not being married.
- **SAINT PATRICK'S DAY**
- **EASTER**—At Easter Day dances, a large cake is exhibited for all to see. Men pay to dance, and the one who dances the most "takes the cake." This expression here refers to a person who dances more than anyone else.
- **MAY DAY**—A folk festival that was celebrated before Christianity and is still celebrated with maypole dancing and flower gathering. Bushes are decorated with flowers or eggshells, which are symbols of life. There is plenty of dancing and singing.

Do you like my fairy costume?

SUMMER

- **BONFIRE NIGHT**—Originally, animal and human bones were burned to appease the gods on Bonfire, or Bone Fire, Night. Later, Bonfire Night became a celebration of the eternal flame of Saint Patrick on the shortest night of the year. Now it is celebrated with dancing and storytelling around the fire.
- **MIDSUMMER'S EVE**—Watch out for fairies this night. They are out to steal mortal brides for themselves. All girls should be kept indoors!
- **MIDSUMMER'S DAY**—Country fairs are held with dancing and singing.
- **ORANGE DAY PARADE**
- **LUGHNASA**—Traditionally, the beginning of the harvest was celebrated with festivities dedicated to the pre-Christian god Lugh [LOO].
- **PUCK'S FAIR**

AUTUMN

Don't you think our maypole looks colorful? Come dance with us!

- ✪ **AUTUMN HARVEST FESTIVAL**—Farmers bring their harvests to town to trade or sell. Potatoes are used to make *poteen* [POT-cheen], a drink that is sold at fairs. People get very jolly. There is lots of dancing and singing, music, and storytelling.
- ✪ **SAMHAIN**
- ✪ **NOVEMBER EVE**—A night when fairies are said to appear. The fairies are sad on this night because they open the graves of the dead and dance with ghosts on the graveyard tombstones. They also try to capture a mortal musician to play for them.
- ✪ **SAINT MARTIN'S DAY**—A Celtic tradition was to kill animals on this day as food for the winter. A little rooster's blood was sprinkled on the doors of houses to keep evil spirits away. Today, farmers put religious medals in all four corners of their fields.

WINTER

- ✪ **CHRISTMAS**
- ✪ **SAINT STEPHEN'S DAY**—Celtic myth had it that the robin (representing the New Year) killed the wren (representing the Old Year) during this time. Wren Boys blacken their faces and go from house to house asking for money to bury the wren. The money they collect is used to buy food and drink for the "wren dance" held on this night.
- ✪ **SAINT BRIGID'S DAY**

Onward march we go! Come follow us!

7

SAINT BRIGID'S DAY

I n the old days, February 1st was considered the start of the growth season. After Christianity was introduced, Saint Brigid (Bridie) was honored instead of the pagan gods. The success of agriculture depended on her intercession. Thus, her feast day was celebrated with reverence and still is today.

Dandelions in full bloom.

Sold into slavery

This very popular female patron saint of Ireland was a fifth century nun who is credited with founding the first convent in Ireland.

Brigid had her beginnings as a slave. Born in Ireland, she was sold into slavery by her own father. When she was freed, she returned to her father voluntarily as a serving girl. She milked cows and made butter. She is also said to have woven the first piece of cloth in Ireland and so became the patron saint of weavers and spinners. Even when she became the head of a **monastery**, she kept doing the things she loved best, such as reaping and making butter.

Left: A ewe and two lambs taking a walk. Do you have animals like these in your country?

Opposite: Wearing masks and visiting homes are all part of the celebrations for Saint Brigid's Day.

Stories about Saint Brigid

This is Saint Brigid's well. It is a holy place where people pray to Bridie, honoring her. Rosary beads or strips of cloth are left there as a remembrance of the visit.

On Saint Brigid's Day people cannot work on anything that involves spinning, digging, or turning a wheel because "Saint Brigid's Day is free from twistings." This way the feast day can be a holiday for the farmers.

Perhaps Saint Brigid was able to place her foot in water or dip her finger in the brook on February 1st, because the first good weather was thought to arrive on this day. As the Irish say, this was the day when "away went the hen that hatches the cold (winter)."

Brigid's feast day is associated with the promise of spring, warmth, new grass, lambs, and milk. The dandelion is known as the Plant of the Bride (from "Bridie") because it yields a milky juice believed to have nourished young spring lambs.

"Brigid's Cloak" or "brat bhride" [BRAT-bridee] was a woven cloth left on the doorstep outside on the eve of Brigid's feast day. During the night the cloth was believed to acquire special healing powers. People would place the cloth around the necks of sick animals to help them get well.

The custom of having women propose marriage to men during a Leap Year can also be traced to Saint Brigid, who persuaded Saint Patrick to grant women that right one year out of every four.

Spinning away at the wheel! Look at how much raw wool there is in the basket!

Feast Day

February 1st is the Feast Day of Saint Brigid, and in many places in rural Ireland people still make Brigid Crosses to honor her. Pageants take place at schools and churches with young women carrying green rushes.

On the eve of Saint Brigid's Day, crosses are woven of rushes and hung for a year above the doors of houses and barns. These crosses are believed to protect the house and the livestock from harm and fire. No evil spirit can pass these charms.

A small folk play is enacted in which a girl playing the part of Brigid brings rushes to the door and is allowed inside. She blesses the family, eats with them, and helps them make crosses.

This man is making Saint Brigid's crosses from straw. After the making of the crosses on the eve of Saint Brigid's feast day, apple griddle cakes are eaten as a tradition.

PUCK'S FAIR

Every year in August, the people of Killorglin in County Kerry busily prepare for a three-day fair. For hundreds of years this town has been the center for a **livestock** fair that has become a major tourist attraction.

Crowning of a billy goat

On Gathering Day when stalls are opened to sell food and drink, and booths are opened for trade and **barter**, a large billy goat is decorated with ribbons and paraded through the streets. He is crowned "King of the Fair" and placed on a three-story platform (his throne) in the town square, where he presides over the fair for three days!

Opposite (top): Look at the little girl crowning the goat during the procession. According to a tale, when the Killorglin Fair first started, the only animal brought there was a billy goat. It was made the fair's symbol because the townsfolk were so grateful. This "crowning" then made the fair attractive to other people who traded in animals.

Left: Look at these two girls enjoying a pony ride at Puck's Fair in Killorglin. Have you ever ridden a pony?

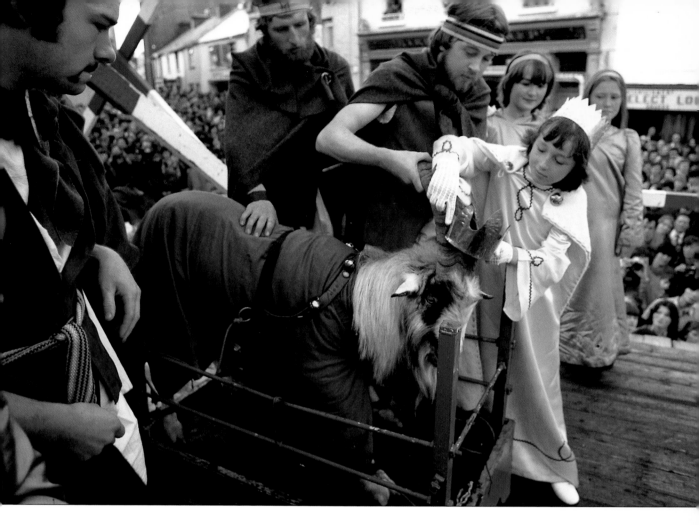

Stories about King Puck

Many people believe the goat is the most perceptive of all animals and that it can even see the wind. That is why the goat is king of the fair.

Hundreds of years ago when the Normans held goat fairs, or puck fairs, a goat was "enthroned" to show that the market was in progress. The popular explanation given for the origin of the Killorglin fair is that English soldiers **plundered** the area long ago. Seeing this happen, a billy goat collected all the farm animals and led them up a mountain for safety. He was crowned king of the fair to honor his bravery.

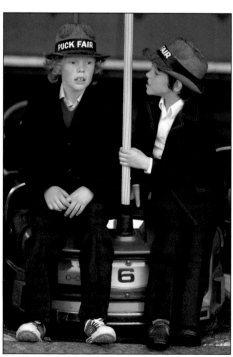

Here are two boys resting on the dodgems. These are small electric cars found at fairs. Driving in an enclosed area, you can either knock into somebody or move away.

It takes a powerful pair of lungs to make music at the fair!

Campfire music

Another name for the gypsies is Travelers. They have their homes in gaily-colored caravans or wagons, and they travel from place to place. At Killorglin, they camp the caravans along the road. At night, they light great campfires and play Irish music. You can hear reels, **jigs**, hornpipes, airs, marches, and old Irish waltzes.

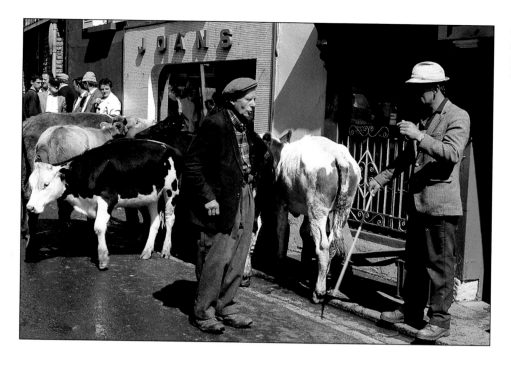

Both people and animals enjoy a sunny day at Puck's Fair.

Gypsies join in

The second day of the fair features a livestock show. Gypsies in large numbers have attended this fair for hundreds of years. They sell and trade horses, donkeys, wagons, and carts.

Scattering Day

Wouldn't you like to take a ride in this horse-drawn carriage, too?

On the evening of the third day, King Puck is led out of town by a piper to the accompaniment of traditional Irish music. This signifies the end of the fair.

Think about this

Puck is the Old Norman word for a mischievous **sprite**, goblin, or elf. It's also a word for the devil. The hair from a goat's whiskers or a goat's foot is believed to drive away evil spirits.

SAINT PATRICK'S DAY

Every year on March 17th, the Irish people honor their patron saint, Patrick, who is also known as Saint Pat or Paddy. His symbol is a shamrock, so the Irish wear shamrocks on his day. They attend special religious services and have community and family gatherings as well. Colorful parades pass through towns and cities led by brass and pipe bands.

Kidnapped by pirates

When Paddy was a young boy of 16, he lived in the British countryside. Pirates from across the Irish Sea kidnapped him, brought him to Erin (Ireland's poetic name), and sold him as a slave. For six years he was a shepherd in the mountains. Finally he escaped and went to a monastery in Europe, where he trained to become a priest in the Roman Catholic Church. After many years he became a bishop, and in A.D. 432, when he was about 60 years old, he returned to Erin to be a missionary to the pagan Celts. He spent the rest of his life doing missionary work.

The shamrock belongs to the clover family of plants. Look at the shamrocks painted on the faces of this happy pair!

Left: This man is dressed as Saint Patrick. The real Saint Patrick is credited with bringing the warm weather for planting, otherwise known as "turning up the warm side of the stone."

Below: A smiling girl enjoys herself. See how warmly she is bundled up.

Miracle man

Ireland was a wild place until Saint Patrick arrived. He traveled the country teaching Christianity and converting the pagans. He gradually changed the pagan festivals into Holy Days, and created many holy places for people to worship God. He built monasteries and churches. He also performed many good and charitable works and even a few miracles!

The shamrock

The shamrock is a small, three-leafed plant that appears in the middle of a season the Celts called Growth. Patrick used the three leaves on one stem to explain the **Holy Trinity** (three persons in one God) to the Celtic tribes.

Legends about Saint Patrick

One tale about Saint Patrick involves a family who refused to be hospitable to him when he appeared at their door. They sent him to the stable to sleep. The next morning, all that remained of the house and its occupants was a hole in the ground! Patrick was annoyed at his mistreatment and caused the house and its family to disappear. Perhaps this is why the Irish people are known today for their hospitality.

Top: These smiling faces show the fun and excitement of celebrating Saint Patrick's Day!

Left: How long do you think it takes to paint a shamrock on your forehead?

Saint Pat's celebration

People all over the world celebrate Saint Patrick's Day on March 17th. There are parades during the day and special dinners at night of corned beef and cabbage, traditional Irish fare. People wear green clothing, badges, buttons, or ribbons on that day because green is the color of the shamrock and the Emerald Isle. This custom is called the wearing of the green. Some people even drink beer that has been dyed green with food coloring. It is also a tradition to have a drink of Patrick's Pot (whiskey) on his feast day. Years ago, people put a sprig of shamrock in their whiskey; this way, they could "drown the shamrock."

In the evening, people meet up at neighborhood pubs to eat and drink, sing Irish folk songs, dance Irish jigs, and tell stories and legends.

Think about this
The largest parade in Ireland to celebrate Saint Patrick takes place in Dublin, but the biggest parade of all is held in New York City. It dates back to 1762. Boston has an even older parade that started in 1737. Can you imagine why this would be?

The largest parade in Ireland— Saint Patrick's Day in Dublin. Huge crowds gather to see the floats and bands.

SAMHAIN

O n October 31st, children dress up in costumes, wear masks, and carry lighted lanterns from house to house to receive treats or play tricks. The lanterns are often carved out of turnips, with scary faces and candles inside. Pumpkin lanterns are also popular.

Below: Adults seem to enjoy dressing up in costumes as much as the children do! Can you identify the character each adult is dressed up as?

Ghosts and goblins

Samhain was the Celtic New Year. This festival began when the Celts lived in Ireland and honored Saman [SHAM-an], the Lord of the Dead. They believed that the souls of people who had died the year before gathered at this time. Being greatly fearful, they used magic to lay evil spirits to rest. People thought the evil spirits would grab anyone found roaming after dark, so they carried fiery torches and disguised themselves with masks and costumes.

The saints come marching in

In 834 Pope Gregory IV made Samhain into a church festival honoring all saints. It was called Hallowmas. All Saint's Day fell on November 1st, so October 31st was All Hallow's Eve, which eventually became Halloween.

Opposite: To the Celts, "The Fires of Peace" occurred when people carried fire torches and went to houses to rid them of evil spirits. Here, the crowd enjoys a different type of fire.

Snapping at apples

Children call this festival Snap Apple Night because they save the best apples from the harvest for games such as bobbing for apples, spearing apples in tubs of water, and trying to bite apples swinging from the rafters by strings. Hazelnuts, which the Celts associated with knowledge and which were used in fortune-telling, are collected from trees, cracked, and eaten on this night. A popular dish served during this festival is Boxty [BOX-tee], which resembles a pancake and is made from potatoes.

Above: Bobbing for apples can be a lot of fun, but it is a lot harder than it looks!

Right: This little girl is trying to eat an apple on a string during Halloween. Do you like apples?

Fancy Dress and Fireworks

For children today, Halloween is a time for fancy dress parties and fireworks. It is also an opportunity for friends and relatives to get together for a meal and perhaps some playful fortune-telling. Traditional dishes are apple tart and barmbrack [BAM-brak], a type of fruit loaf.

Wow! Have you ever seen a mask this big? How heavy do you think it is?

Think about this
Myths are much more than just make-believe tales. They are the remnants of ideas humans once lived by. Many old myths survive as festivals for young people. Halloween is an example.

ORANGE DAY

I f you are a Protestant living in Northern Ireland, you probably have a friend or relative who is a member of the Orange Society. Each year on July 12th, the Orangemen hold a parade. People gather to listen to religious and political speeches.

Orange lilies

Orange Day is the anniversary of the Battle of the Boyne, which took place in Ireland in July of 1690. The trouble began when James II, a Roman Catholic king, lost his throne to William of Orange, who was a Protestant. Each side raised an army of about 30,000 men, and they fought on the banks of the Boyne River. The Protestants won the battle, but the Catholics formed "**underground societies**" to restore the line of James. The Protestants formed the Orange Order to maintain links with England. William of Orange became a hero to all Protestants.

Orangemen abroad

The Loyal Orange Institute was organized in 1795 in Ulster, a region in Northern Ireland. Orangemen support Protestant Christianity and civil and religious freedom. They meet regularly in groups called **lodges**. Many Irish Protestants who have moved away from Ireland have set up lodges in their new countries—mainly England, Scotland, Canada, and the United States—and still celebrate Orange Day on July 12th.

Left: This is what William of Orange looked like. When he fought in battle, he wore a spray of orange lilies as his symbol. Today, the orange lily remains his symbol.

Opposite: The Orange Day Parade in Belfast. Besides having orange lilies pinned to their clothing, the marchers also wear orange sashes. They march to stirring music and carry banners.

THINGS FOR YOU TO DO

Do you wonder what Gaelic sounds like? Here is your chance to find out! Try learning how to say the days of the week and some numbers in Gaelic.

Speak Gaelic

The Celts' language has lasted for 2,000 years in Ireland. Today, Irish people speak English and Gaelic, the language handed down from the Celts. Here are some words you can practice. If you meet someone from Ireland, you can surprise him or her by speaking Gaelic.

Days of the week

Monday	*Luan [LOO-in]*
Tuesday	*Mairt [MARTCH]*
Wednesday	*Ceadaoin [KAY-deen]*
Thursday	*Deardaoin [JEYR-deen]*
Friday	*Aoine [HAYN-ya]*
Saturday	*Sathairn [sa-HARN]*
Sunday	*Domhnach [DOW-neg]*

Numbers

One	*Aon [AYN]*
Two	*Do [DAU]*
Three	*Tri [TREE]*
Four	*Ceathar [KE-har]*
Five	*Cuig [KOO-ig]*
Six	*Se [SHAY]*
Seven	*Seacht [SHAKT]*
Eight	*Ocht [OKHT]*
Nine	*Naci [NEE]*
Ten	*Deich [JEYKH]*

Exercise your vocal cords!

Do you enjoy music? Here is a short song for you to sing. If you have a friend who plays the piano or the guitar, you can try out this song together. You might even want to perform this piece for your family after dinner!

Cut the Loaf

When I was young I had no sense, I bought a wee fid-dle for eigh-teen pence, And all the tune that I could play was cut the loaf and ate a-way.

Things to look for in your library

The Book of Holidays Around the World. Alice van Straalen (E.P. Dutton, 1986).
Children of the Salmon and Other Irish Folktales. Eileen O'Faolain (Atlantic Little Brown).
Ireland Is My Home (My Home Country). Gini Holland (Gareth Stevens, 1993).
The Legend of Finn McCoul. (Animated by Rabbit Ears Productions, 1991).
Lucky Leprechaun's Lane. (citylink@neosoft.com, 1997).
Myth, Legend and Romance. Dr. D. O'Hogain (Prentice-Hall Press, 1991).
The Republic of Ireland—Enchantment of the World. Dennis B. Fradin (Children's Press, 1984).
A Wee Bit of Fun. (webmaster@nando.net, 1997).
A World of Festivals—A Day for Being Irish. (Beringer Films, 1990).

MAKE A SHAMROCK NECKLACE

M ake your own shamrock to wear on Saint Patrick's Day. The shamrock is the symbol for Ireland. The green is the color of the beautiful Emerald Isle.

1

2

3

5

6

4

8

7

9

You will need:
1. A paint tray
2. Paints of different colors
3. A paintbrush
4. Some modeling clay
5. A paper cutter
6. A rolling pin
7. A bowl of water
8. Sequins
9. Threads of different colors.

1 Flatten the clay using the rolling pin.

2 Cut out the shape of a shamrock with your paper cutter. Poke a hole at the top of your clay shamrock with the end of your paintbrush.

3 Wait for the clay to dry. Paint the shamrock any color you want and wait for that to dry.

4 Decorate your clay shamrock with sequins. Pull a piece of thread through the hole on the shamrock and tie the ends together.

MAKE SHAMROCK COOKIES

The Irish people grow lots of potatoes, and many Irish recipes include them. They are a staple of the Irish diet. These cookies will help you and your family celebrate Saint Patrick's Day. If you like nuts and raisins, you can add a half cup (60 g) of each to the cookie batter.

You will need:

1. 1¼ cups (300 g) hot, cooked potatoes
2. ½ cup (100 g) sugar
3. ¼ cup (60 ml) honey
4. 7 ounces (200 g) butter or margarine
5. 1 cup (140 g) all-purpose flour
6. 2 teaspoons baking powder
7. 1 teaspoon ground cinnamon or ground allspice
8. ¼ teaspoon ground cloves
9. ½ teaspoon grated nutmeg
10. ½ teaspoon salt
11. 1 egg for brushing
12. Green sprinkles
13. A large bowl
14. A wooden spoon
15. Measuring spoons
16. Measuring cups
17. A sieve
18. A kitchen glove
19. A small cooking brush
20. A metal tray
21. A teaspoon
22. A potato masher

1 Place the hot, cooked potatoes in a large bowl and mash them thoroughly.

2 Cream the sugar, syrup, and butter together. Beat in the mashed potatoes.

3 Sift together the flour, baking powder, spices, and salt. Add sifted, dry ingredients to the batter to make dough. Mix until it is smooth.

4 Using a teaspoon, drop three small mounds of dough close together to form the shape of a shamrock on a lightly greased cookie sheet.

5 Brush the tops of the cookies with some lightly beaten egg. Top with green sprinkles and bake for 20 minutes at 375°F (190°C). This recipe makes 40 cookies or more, so you can invite your friends over to share them.

GLOSSARY

barter, 12 — To trade or exchange one object for another.

Celts, 4 — The early settlers in Ireland who arrived before Christianity.

Holy Trinity, 17 — The Christian belief of Father, Son, and Holy Spirit as three beings in one God.

jig, 14 — The music that goes along with a folk dance that is characterized by kicking and leaping.

leprechaun, 4 — A mischievous elf in Irish folklore, sometimes called the elves' shoemaker.

livestock, 12 — Animals such as horses and sheep that are kept on a farm.

lodge, 24 — The meeting place for a group of men with the same interests, such as the Orangemen.

monastery, 8 — A place where people who join religious orders live and work.

plunder, 13 — To steal or loot, as pirates do, or as in a war.

sprite, 15 — An elf or fairy.

underground society, 24 — A group of people who meet secretly.

INDEX